Spring Harvest Bible Workbook

JONAH

God's Compassion

First published in 2003 Spring Harvest Publishing Division and Authentic Lifestyle

10 09 08 07 06 05 04   8 7 6 5 4 3 2

Reprinted in 2004 by Authentic Media

9 Holdom Avenue, Bletchley, Milton Keynes, Bucks., MK1 1QR, UK

and P.O. Box 1047, Waynesboro, GA 30830-2047, USA

www.authenticmedia.co.uk

British Library Cataloguing in Publication Data

A catalogue record for this book is available from the British Library

ISBN 1-85078-508-2

Typeset by Spring Harvest
Cover design by Diane Bainbridge
Printed in Great Britain by Bell and Bain Ltd., Glasgow

CONTENTS

About this book   4

Introduction to Jonah   7

Session One: Running away from God   8

Session Two: When pagans set the standard   12

Session Three: Prayer works   16

Session Four: True repentance   20

Session Five: God's character   24

Session Six: God's mission   28

Leaders' Guide Introduction   33

Session One: notes   37

Session Two: notes   38

Session Three: notes   40

Session Four: notes   41

Session Five: notes   43

Session Six: notes   44

Further reading   47

ABOUT THIS BOOK

This book is written primarily for a group situation, but can easily be used by individuals who want to study the life of the prophet Jonah. It can be used in a variety of contexts, so it is perhaps helpful to spell out the assumptions that we have made about the groups that will use it. These can have a variety of names – homegroups, Bible study groups, cell groups – we've used housegroup as the generic term.

▶ The emphasis of the studies will be on the application of the Bible. Group members will not just learn facts, but will be encouraged to think 'How does this apply to me? What change does it require of me? What incidents or situations in my life is this relevant to?'

▶ Housegroups can encourage honesty and make space for questions and doubts. The aim of the studies is not to find the 'right answer', but to help members understand the Bible by working through their questions. The Christian faith throws up paradoxes. Events in people's lives may make particular verses difficult to understand. The housegroup should be a safe place to express these concerns.

▶ Housegroups can give opportunities for deep friendships to develop. Group members will be encouraged to talk about their experiences, feelings, questions, hopes and fears. They will be able to offer one another pastoral support and to get involved in each other's lives.

▶ There is a difference between being a collection of individuals who happen to meet together every Wednesday and being an effective group who bounce ideas off each other, spark inspiration and creativity, pooling their talents and resources to create solutions together: one whose whole is definitely greater than the sum of its parts. The process of working through these studies will encourage healthy group dynamics.

Space is given for you to write answers, comments, questions and thoughts. This book will not tell you what to think, but will help you discover the truth of God's word through thinking, discussing, praying and listening.

FOR GROUP MEMBERS

▶ You will probably get more out of the study if you spend some time during the week reading the passage and thinking about the questions. Make a note of anything you don't understand.

▶ Pray that God will help you to understand the passage and show you how to apply it. Pray for other members in the group too, that they will find the study helpful.

▶ Be willing to take part in the discussions. The leader of the group is not there as an expert with all the answers. They will want everyone to get involved and share their thoughts and opinions.

▶ However, don't dominate the group! If you are aware that you are saying a lot, make space for others to contribute. Be sensitive to other group members and aim to be encouraging. If you disagree with someone, say so but without putting down their contribution.

FOR INDIVIDUALS

▶ Although this book is written with a group in mind, it can also easily be used by individuals. You obviously won't be able to do the group activities suggested, but you can consider how you would answer the questions and write your thoughts in the space provided.

▶ You may find it helpful to talk to a prayer partner about what you have learnt, and ask them to pray for you as you try and apply what you are learning to your life.

▶ The New International Version of the text is printed in the book. If you use a different version, then read from your own Bible as well.

Other titles in this Spring Harvest Bible Studies series:

Sermon on the Mount – ISBN 1-85078-407-8
Based on the Spring Harvest 2000 theme, King of the Hill.

Jesus at the Centre – ISBN 1-85078-440-X
Based on the Spring Harvest 2001 theme, A Royal Banquet.

Letters to the Churches – ISBN 1-85078-441-8
Based on the Spring Harvest 2002 theme, You've Got Mail.

Big Themes from Colossians – ISBN 1-85078-457-4
Based on the Spring Harvest 1999 theme, Across the Borderline.

Mission of God – ISBN 1-85078-496-5
Based on the Spring Harvest 2003 theme, Shepherd's Bush to King's Cross.

David – After God's Own Heart – ISBN 1-85078-497-3
Based on selected chapters from Ian Coffey's book,
The Story of David, ISBN 1-85078-485-X.

Moses – Friend of God – ISBN 1-85078-519-8
Studies on Moses.

Connect! Workbook – ISBN 1-85078-521-X
Based on Tim Jeffery and Steve Chalke's ground-breaking book rethinking
mission for the 21st century.

INTRODUCTION TO JONAH

Jonah was one of the most successful prophets in the Old Testament.

He had a more glamorous brief than prophets like Isaiah or Jeremiah because his job was to predict victories for Israel. As Jonah's prophesies came true and the nation's borders expanded, he became a hero. Under King Jeroboam II, Israel enjoyed great prosperity and political influence.

Life was going well for the prophet until a single mission trip revealed the rotten state of his heart. When the call came to go to Nineveh, Jonah began to realise that God's mission was not just to save Israel but to extend his grace to all people. In theory this was acceptable – until of course that grace extended to Israel's worst enemy, Assyria. One could understand Jonah's reluctance to go to the city of Nineveh because the Assyrians were famous for their cruelty and dirty fighting tactics. But it wasn't so much that Jonah was worried for his safety: he was worried that the people would actually listen to God's message, repent and be saved. Surely Israel's privileged relationship with God couldn't be shared with such wicked people? That God would show mercy in saving the Assyrians was anathema to Jonah.

And so the book of Jonah records a series of 'teachable moments' as God introduces his reluctant prophet to a few life-lessons. God wanted Jonah to learn that his grace and compassion were not confined to the Israelites but extended to a city full of pagans and even to a disenchanted self-important prophet like him. God wanted Jonah to grasp that his love and mercy was limitless and he was free to save whom he chose.

The message of Jonah is that 'Salvation belongs to the Lord!' But God wants us to share his passion for lost people, to see them with his eyes. God invites us to share his mission. Will we play our part?

RUNNING AWAY FROM GOD

AIM: To see the futility of disobeying God

One of the first words a child learns is 'No'. As adults, even as Christians, we often say 'No' to our heavenly Father – if not consciously then at least by our actions. Our disobedience affects us and those around us. Most importantly, it breaks God's heart as he longs for us to trust him enough to obey.

> *The word of the Lord came to Jonah son of Amittai: 'Go to the great city of Nineveh and preach against it, because its wickedness has come up before me.'*
>
> *But Jonah ran away from the Lord and headed for Tarshish. He went down to Joppa, where he found a ship bound for that port. After paying the fare, he went aboard and sailed for Tarshish to flee from the Lord.*
>
> *Then the Lord sent a great wind on the sea, and such a violent storm arose that the ship threatened to break up. All the sailors were afraid and each cried out to his own god. And they threw the cargo into the sea to lighten the load.*
>
> *But Jonah had gone down below deck, where he lay down and fell into a deep sleep. The captain went to him and said, 'How can you sleep? Get up and call on your god! Maybe he will take notice of us, and we will not perish.'*

Jonah 1:1–6

TO SET THE SCENE
As you get to know the others in your group, invite people to share some childhood memories of times when they flouted authority. This could be a light-hearted look at their upbringing or school days.

Do some background work.

1 What can you find out about Nineveh? Look at Jonah 3:8, 4:11, Nahum 3:1–4, 16–17, 19.

2 Where was Tarshish? Use a Bible atlas to find where this city was in relation to where God wanted Jonah to go.

3 In verse 3, the thought that Jonah was running away from the Lord is repeated. How did other prophets respond when God's word came to them? Look at Amos 3:8, Isaiah 6:1–8, Numbers 22:38. How is Jonah's response unusual?

Read Jonah 1:1–6

4 Jonah 1:1 says 'The word of the Lord came to Jonah...' How does God's word come to us today?

5 Despite hearing God's word so clearly, Jonah chose to disobey. What was his reason (look at Jon. 4:2)?

6 Surely God's prophet would know it was futile to oppose God's plans. Scan through the book and find the examples where God takes the initiative to accomplish his plans and bring his wayward prophet into line.

7 Jonah's disobedience brought trouble to himself as well as the sailors.
   a) Even though we know the futility of disobedience, why do we still do it?
   b) How has your disobedience affected others?

8 When God speaks to us he expects obedience – even when we can't see the big picture (Jon. 1: 1–2). For example, look at Genesis 6:9–22, 22:1–18. Why do you think these Old Testament characters chose to obey God? What lessons can we learn?

9 a) What holds you back from sharing the gospel with others?

   b) What practical measures can you take to overcome your fears and concerns?

10 As a church in our generation, do we run away from the call of God to take the gospel into all the world – including the Ninevehs?

The church is the church only when it exists for others.

Dietrich Bonhoeffer

WORSHIP

Begin with a silent time of confession. Confess the times you have heard God's voice and been disobedient, the times you've run away from sharing the gospel in your Nineveh. Together praise God for Jesus – the ultimate prophet; the one who was obedient to God despite the cost, the one who said 'Not my will but yours be done.' In twos, share together the areas of your life where you have to start saying to God, 'Not my will but yours.' Pray for each other.

FURTHER STUDY

To find out how you and your church could be more involved in your own local 'Ninevehs', speak to your minister or church leaders. The organisations listed at the back of this workbook may also be able to give you some suggestions to help you get started.

FOR NEXT WEEK

Jonah 1:1 says 'The word of the Lord came to Jonah...' Ask God to speak to you this week and be willing to be obedient. Pray specifically for opportunities to share the gospel and be ready to take them!

ACTIVITY PAGE

We may wish we could share the gospel like Billy Graham or the Apostle Paul but, for many of us, even the most basic spiritual conversation with a non-Christian brings us out in a hot flush of embarrassment. We get tongue-tied and hopelessly self-conscious. We will never be able to prepare ourselves fully for these 'gospel conversations' as each one will be unique, responding to the questions and needs of the other person, but perhaps the following exercises will help us gain confidence and think through some possible answers.

Divide into two groups.

Have the individuals in one group work on their testimonies. Think about your testimony in terms of life before your conversion, how you became a Christian and what has happened since, the difference it has made to your life.

Encourage each person to read their testimony out to the group. Comment on:
▶ The elements that would have been helpful to a non-Christian
▶ Was there any Christian jargon that has to be removed?

Have the individuals in the other group discuss how they would introduce the gospel in the following scenarios. For each case study, think though the key elements of the gospel and how they should be presented.

▶ You have just got a part-time job at a local school and you're talking with the deputy-head. She mentions that her husband has a 'faith'.
▶ Jehovah's Witnesses knock on your door, offering you their magazine.
▶ You're at the school gate waiting for your child and a single mum strikes up a conversation with you. She admits that she's tired and stressed and wishes there was someone who could help.
▶ After months of unemployment you've just got a job as an accountant in a small firm. The owner asks you to fudge the books. When you explain that you can't because you're a Christian, he replies that he's a Christian too.

Of course the best preparation for introducing people to God is to know him well yourself. Spend time with him in prayer and reading his word, so you can discern his voice leading you in these conversations and you can speak his words to others.

WHEN PAGANS SET THE STANDARD

AIM: To increase our spiritual sensitivity to God's will and work

We've probably all experienced those embarrassing moments when a non-Christian or very new Christian has shown more integrity or honesty than us. Then we wish, as the Americans say, that we had 'walked the talk'. Let's use those experiences as a spur to greater spiritual sensitivity and obedience.

Then the sailors said to each other, 'Come, let us cast lots to find out who is responsible for this calamity.' They cast lots and the lot fell on Jonah.

So they asked him, 'Tell us, who is responsible for making all this trouble for us? What do you do? Where do you come from? What is your country? From what people are you?'

He answered, 'I am a Hebrew and I worship the Lord, the God of heaven, who made the sea and the land.'

This terrified them and they asked, 'What have you done?' (They knew he was running away from the Lord, because he had already told them so.)

The sea was getting rougher and rougher. So they asked him, 'What should we do to you to make the sea calm down for us?'

'Pick me up and throw me into the sea,' he replied, 'and it will become calm. I know that it is my fault that this great storm has come upon you.'

Instead, the men did their best to row back to land. But they could not, for the sea grew wilder than before. Then they cried to the Lord, 'O Lord, please do not let us die for taking this man's life. Do not hold us accountable for killing an innocent man, for you, O Lord, have done as you pleased.'

Then they took Jonah and threw him overboard, and the raging sea grew calm. At this the men greatly feared the Lord, and they offered a sacrifice to the Lord and made vows to him.

But the Lord provided a great fish to swallow Jonah, and Jonah was inside the fish three days and three nights.

Jonah 1:7–17

TO SET THE SCENE

A quiz to test your sensitivity!

▶ Do you cry at sad movies?
▶ Would a row with a friend keep you awake at night?
▶ Can you tell when your spouse or someone close to you is upset without them saying a word?

What criteria do we use to check our spiritual sensitivity to God?

Read Jonah 1:1–17

1 Look at the behaviour of Jonah and the captain of the ship. What are the contrasts?

2 In what ways were the sailors more spiritually sensitive to God than Jonah?

Look at:
▶ Their beliefs about preserving life
▶ Their willingness to pray

3 What do you make of Jonah's response in v9?

WHAT DOES SEARCH THE BIBLE SAY?

4 At times we too say the right things without doing them, or even do the right things without meaning them. How do passages like Matthew 25:31–46, Micah 6: 6–8, and Isaiah 29:13 challenge you?

HOW DOES THIS APPLY TO ME

5 How can we become more integrated Christians, where what we say ties up with what we do?

6 Despite Jonah's disobedience God gave him a second chance (v17). What does that tell you about God's view of our failures?

7 God showed his mercy and grace by rescuing Jonah as well as the sailors. Share in twos the ways you have seen God's mercy and grace in your own life.

HOW DOES THIS
APPLY TO ME

8 We will keep on failing but how can we increase our spiritual sensitivity to God?

WORSHIP

When the sailors realised that God was in control of this situation, they cried out 'You, O Lord, have done as you pleased' (v14). They offered a sacrifice and made vows to him (v16). Spend time reflecting what God has been saying to you through this study.

▶ Is there a situation in your life that you need to write over 'You, O Lord, have done as you pleased'?
▶ Is there a vow or promise you need to make to God, a particular area of your life you need to give to him?
▶ Is there a sacrifice you need to offer to God, a practical act to show the seriousness of your commitment to him?
▶ Have you realised your disobedience in a particular area and recognised that God is the only one able to rescue you? Ask him to send the big fish of second chances!

FOR NEXT WEEK

Part of the reason we're not spiritually sensitive to God must be that we don't listen to him enough! Our prayer times are often just a list of requests and we rarely wait for God to speak to us. This week, schedule some time when you can learn to listen to God's voice. Read a passage of Scripture, meditate on God's word and then wait for him to speak. It may take some time to discern his voice but just be still!

ACTIVITY PAGE

In many instances pagans still set the standards for society because we are too wrapped up in our own church ministries to interact with them.

Think about your locality and what is going on in the wider world scene. Is there an issue that you should be raising a concern about? Somewhere you could help? How best could a Christian voice be heard?

▶   Should you write a letter to your MP and the Prime Minister?
▶   Should you speak to someone in the local authority?
▶   Should you write to the television companies to complain about a particular TV programme? Or indeed to praise one?
▶   Should you start a prayer group for the local school?
▶   Should you run for a local council/school board post?
▶   Should you support organisations that put Bibles into hospitals, hotels and prisons?

On some issues it might be helpful to speak to your church leaders to see if you can have the support of the whole church.

PRAYER WORKS

 AIM: To make prayer a priority

When there are national disasters, Prime Ministers and Presidents call for prayer: when bad things happen to friends and family, we're quick to say 'Our prayers are with you.' In an emergency, God suddenly becomes everyone's best friend. But what priority does prayer have in our everyday routine when things are going well? Most of us would admit it doesn't have a high enough priority. And then when we see God answer our prayers, we wonder why we don't pray more!

From inside the fish Jonah prayed to the Lord his God. He said:

"In my distress I called to the Lord, and he answered me.
From the depths of the grave I called for help, and you listened to my cry.
You hurled me into the deep, into the very heart of the seas, and the currents swirled about me; all your waves and breakers swept over me.
I said, 'I have been banished from your sight; yet I will look again towards your holy temple.'
The engulfing waters threatened me, the deep surrounded me; seaweed was wrapped around my head.
To the roots of the mountains I sank down; the earth beneath barred me forever.
But you brought my life up from the pit, O Lord my God.

"When my life was ebbing away, I remembered you, Lord, and my prayer rose to you, to your holy temple.

"Those who cling to worthless idols forfeit the grace that could be theirs.
But I, with a song of thanksgiving, will sacrifice to you.
What I have vowed I will make good. Salvation comes from the Lord."

And the Lord commanded the fish, and it vomited Jonah onto dry land.

Jonah 2:1–10

TO SET THE SCENE

Share together memorable examples of God answering prayer. This could be other people's prayers for you, unexpected answers to prayers or ways in which, even though the situation did not change, God aligned your attitude to his.

Read Jonah 2:1–10

1 How does Jonah describe his nautical experience? What actually happened to him?

2 Some commentators believe that Jonah's prayer was one of true repentance, others do not. Divide into two groups, with each group taking a side in the debate. What evidence can you come up with from the text to support your view?

3 What reminders do your answers to question 2 give about the tone, style and content of our prayers?

Sincerity – God Centred
Backed up with action

4 Where did Jonah believe his prayers were going (2: 4, 7)?

Holy Temple

WHAT DOES **SEARCH** **THE BIBLE SAY?** **5** a) Describe what happens to our words when we pray. Where are our words going? Look at Hebrews 4:14–16, Revelation 5:8. b) How does this make you feel about prayer?

> *If God can do more than all we ask or imagine, why not ask for more imagination?*
>
> **Dave Davidson**

6 'Salvation comes from the Lord' (v9). What does the consequences of that phrase mean for:
   a) Jonah
   b) The Ninevites
   c) Us
   d) Those we witness to

– Free to save people of Nineveh
Calling for Repentance

HOW DOES THIS

APPLY TO ME

7 Like the sailors, Jonah and the Ninevites we are prone to use prayer like a 999 emergency call. What times of the day could you build prayer into your routine? What priorities do you need to shift to give yourself regular times to pray?

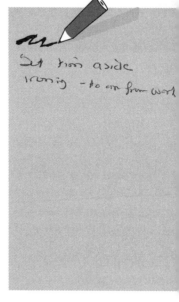

Set him aside
Ironing – to am from work

APPLY THIS TO

MY CHURCH

8 What priority does prayer have in the life of your church?

   a) What could you do promote more prayer in your church?
   b) If your church prayer times need to be improved, what can you do?

The church has many organisers, but few agonisers; many who pay, but few who pray; many resters, but few wrestlers; many who are enterprising, but few who are interceding. That's the difference between the modern church and the early church. In the matter of effective praying, never have so many left so much to so few.

Leonard Ravenhill

WORSHIP

Spend time writing your own prayer to God. Describe your situation to God with the same degree of detail that Jonah did. If it is appropriate, pray your prayers aloud. If not, follow Jonah's example of using the psalms as a basis for your prayers. Read out and pray through some psalms pertinent to the situation of people in your group.

FURTHER STUDY

If you'd like to learn more about how to pray there are various resources available. A good place to start is *Too Busy Not to Pray* by Bill Hybels.

FOR NEXT WEEK

Think of someone you know who has run away from God. It could be a young person away at university, your child or grandchild, a friend or neighbour. They may seem to be blatantly disobeying God but we don't know what is going on in their hearts. Pray that they would cry out to God again and that he would be gracious to them, as he has been with us.

ACTIVITY PAGE

How can prayer be a higher priority in your small group time?

Think through:

▶ Could you change the prayer slot to a better time?
▶ What values need to be held in common by your group to encourage people to share issues for prayer (confidentiality, affirmation etc)?
▶ Do you want to focus on specific projects or people for long-term prayer?
▶ Could someone in the group keep a journal to record requests and answers to prayer? Would you pray for each other more if you knew each other better? How can you achieve this?
▶ Do you need to keep prayers shorter so that more people can pray?

Discuss these issues together and come up with a strategy to give prayer more of an emphasis in your sessions together.

Then pray!

TRUE REPENTANCE

AIM: To realise the urgent need for both Christians and non-Christians to repent before God

'Sorry' is such a hard word to say. We said it more easily as children but as we grow up it tends to stick in our throats a bit more. We become aware of our rights and pride gets in the way. 'Sorry' is especially hard to say to God because it means we've got to get out of the driving seat and give him control – something even Christians find difficult!

Then the word of the Lord came to Jonah a second time: 'Go to the great city of Nineveh and proclaim to it the message I give you.'

Jonah obeyed the word of Lord and went to Nineveh. Now Nineveh was a very important city – a visit required three days. On the first day, Jonah started into the city. He proclaimed: 'Forty days and Nineveh will be overturned.' The Ninevites believed God. They declared a fast, and all of them, from the greatest to the least, put on sackcloth.

When the news reached the king of Nineveh, he rose from his throne, took off his royal robes, covered himself with sackcloth and sat down in the dust. Then he issued a proclamation in Nineveh:

'By the decree of the king and his nobles: Do not let any man or beast, herd or flock, taste anything; do not let them eat or drink. But let man and beast be covered with sackcloth. Let everyone call urgently to God. Let them give up their evil ways and their violence. Who knows? God may yet relent and with compassion turn from his fierce anger so that we will not perish.'

When God saw what they did and how they turned from their evil ways, he had compassion and did not bring upon them the destruction he had threatened.

Jonah 3:1–10

TO SET THE SCENE

How easy do you find it to say 'sorry'?

Would you describe saying 'sorry' as:
   a)   Climbing Mount Everest?
   b)   A ramble in the hills?
   c)   A stroll in the park?

When us the last time you said 'sorry':
   a)   Last week?
   b)   Last month?
   c)   Last year?

If you had a row with a friend or spouse would you:
   a)   Say 'sorry' immediately?
   b)   Sleep on it?
   c)   Give them the silent treatment until they raised the issue?

Read Jonah 3:1–10

ENGAGING WITH THE WORLD

1 How would you explain the word 'repentance' to a non-Christian?

2 How did Jonah and the Ninevites demonstrate true repentance in this chapter?

3 What do we learn about God from these verses? How closely do you mirror these characteristics?

4 What are the benefits and blessings for us when we lead someone to true repentance in Christ?

WHAT DOES THE BIBLE SAY?

5 What should motivate us to share the gospel and encourage people to true repentance? Look up these Bible references for ideas – Matthew 28:19.20; Romans 1:9; 2 Peter 3:10.

6 What is the place of regular repentance and confession in the life of a believer?

APPLY THIS TO
MY CHURCH

7 Think of the church in this country. What are the things the church needs to repent of? How could we show a change of heart and direction?

HOW DOES THIS
APPLY TO ME

8 This chapter demonstrates that when there is true repentance, there is a radical transformation of society. How is our repentance affecting society? In what ways are we like salt and light in our community?

WORSHIP

It may be helpful to leave time for personal repentance. Perhaps have a worship CD playing in the background as individuals speak privately to God. Then light a candle for each of the sins you feel the church universal needs to repent of (look at your answers to question 7). Then pray together that in each of these areas God would enable us to be light in our community, pointing people to the Light of the World.

FOR NEXT WEEK

Repentance involves us not just saying 'sorry' to God but saying 'sorry' to others and asking their forgiveness. Is there someone you need to ask to forgive you this week?

GOD'S CHARACTER

AIM: To appreciate and imitate the character of God

It is easier to live with a made-up caricature of God than the real thing. We can make God into what we want and, not surprisingly, he often ends up looking remarkably like us! One of the secrets of the Christian life is to discover who God truly is and then to worship him, even for the aspects of his character that are difficult to live with.

> *But Jonah was greatly displeased and became very angry. He prayed to the Lord, 'O Lord, is this not what I said when I was still at home? This is why I was so quick to flee to Tarshish. I knew that you are a gracious and compassionate God, slow to anger and abounding in love, a God who relents from sending calamity. Now, O Lord, take away my life, for it is better for me to die than to live.'*
>
> *But the Lord replied, 'Have you any right to be angry?'*
>
> *Jonah went out and sat down at a place east of the city. There he made himself a shelter, sat in its shade and waited to see what would happen to the city.*
>
> *Jonah 4:1–5*

TO SET THE SCENE

Choose another person in the group and on a piece of paper write down three aspects of their character. Take turns reading the character traits out aloud. See if the others can guess who you're describing.

Read Jonah 4:1–5

1 Jonah had gone to preach to Nineveh but his heart wasn't in it. What were the lessons he still hadn't learnt?

→ Did not appreciate Gods compassion →

Friend rather than judge →

2 Although Jonah knew God's character in theory, he didn't like the reality. In what ways are we in danger of living with a caricature of God that is easier to accept than the reality?

3 Knowing God's character and reciting it as he did should have caused Jonah to respond in worship. How does knowledge of God increase your

- a) Private devotions?
- b) Corporate worship?

APPLY THIS TO
MY CHURCH

4 In turn, how can our corporate worship increase our appreciation of the character of God? Think about the activities in your worship services and their content.

HOW DOES THIS
APPLY TO ME

5 God's grace and mercy are an example to us of how to treat others. Brainstorm the reasons why we find it difficult to show grace and mercy to others. Half the group should think about our attitude to Christians and the other half of the group our attitude to non-Christians. Discuss your answers together.

Christians higher expectations -

Non C. judgemental about lifestyles.

6 Jonah found it difficult to serve a God who was sovereign, who had the freedom to act as he chose. Can you identify with him?

Not always do as we wish.

APPLY THIS TO MY CHURCH

7 Jonah wanted God to be only God of the Israelites. Whilst we don't consciously keep God to ourselves often our behaviour sends out a different message.

Think about your church:
a) Is the social/economic make-up reflective of the broader community?
b) How are newcomers made to feel welcome?
c) Do any of your traditions needlessly make newcomers feel uncomfortable?
d) Do you frequently use Christian clichés or make 'in-house' comments?

WORSHIP
Use this worship time to increase your heart knowledge of God as you discussed in question 4 Have an informal time where individuals pray, read passages of Scripture, sing songs or play CDs that focus on the character of God. As you appreciate him again in a fresh way, commit to imitating a specific aspect of his character that you need to reflect more.

FURTHER STUDY
There are many resources available that address the character of God and how we can become more like him. Two books worth looking at are J.I. Packer's *Knowing God* and Max Lucado's *Just like Jesus*.

FOR NEXT WEEK
Think of the characteristics of God. Which one do you need to emulate more? Which aspects of God's character do you need to respect rather than resist? Put practical steps in place to show your change of heart this week.

GOD'S MISSION

AIM: To understand and share in God's mission to a lost world

What do you think are the most highly regarded qualities in our generation – tolerance, patience, a desire to succeed ...? Whatever your views, 'independence' is probably on your list somewhere. Independence is considered to be a mark of maturity. Even as Christians, we try to be independent. We claim to love God but often live by our own agendas, instead of trying to please him. We need to learn to stop and ask God what he has a burden for, where he is working, and then give up our plans to join him.

> Then the Lord God provided a vine and made it grow up over Jonah to give shade for his head to ease his discomfort, and Jonah was very happy about the vine. But at dawn the next day God provided a worm, which chewed the vine so that it withered. When the sun rose, God provided a scorching east wind, and the sun blazed on Jonah's head so that he grew faint. He wanted to die, and said 'It would be better for me to die than to live.'
>
> But God said to Jonah, 'Do you have a right to be angry about the vine?'
>
> 'I do' he said. 'I am angry enough to die.'
>
> But the Lord said, 'You have been concerned about this vine, though you did not tend it or make it grow. It sprang up overnight and died overnight. But Nineveh has more than a hundred and twenty thousand people who cannot tell their right hand from their left, and many cattle as well. Should I not be concerned about that great city?'
>
> *Jonah 4:6–11*

TO SET THE SCENE

Split into twos with your partner or someone else you know reasonably well in the group and answer the following questions on each other's behalf, without conferring. Then compare answers. How well do you know your friend?

▶ What is their favourite colour/flower/meal?
▶ What would be their dream holiday?
▶ If they could meet any celebrity, who would it be?

Do you agree with each other's answers? How well do you know each other's interests and desires?

Read Jonah 4:4-11

1 What was God's point with his nature lesson?

> *First think WOW with God for missions. The HOW will follow. Never think HOW before WOW.*
> ### Dan and Dave Davidson

2 What do we learn about Jonah from the fact he repeated his death wish three times in chapter 4?

3 Writing mission statements is popular in the secular world and in our churches. Brainstorm together what you think God's mission statement would be. Would there be any verse in the Bible God would use to sum up his activity in the world?

 APPLY THIS TO MY CHURCH **4** Write a list of all the activities that your church is involved in. How do these activities square with God's mission statement? Do they need to be changed in any way or given a different emphasis to bring them more in line with God's mission?

- Coffee Morning
Ben said we should advertise -
More Goangelistic.
Toddler Group

5 Every Christian should be a world Christian. Robin Thomas gives three characteristics by which you can measure yourself. Are you:

- ▶ Committed to God's purpose for the world
- ▶ Committed to God's people who are to carry out his purpose
- ▶ Committed to working out his purpose in daily life

Using these three traits as a guide on a scale of 1–10, (1 being poor and 10 being excellent) how much of a world Christian do you think you are? In what areas do you need to improve?

6 In twos, share with each other what you feel your part in God's mission is. Have you identified a mission-field? How are you spreading the good news?

Questions to conclude this series

7 What are the main themes of the book of Jonah?

God's Love, Forgiveness

8 What have you personally learnt about God and about yourself from this study? How can you make these new things part of your daily life?

> *We are the sixty-seventh book of the Bible. People read our lives, our actions and our words and believe that they know what being a Christian means.*
>
> **Bryant L Myers**

WORSHIP

Give people time to respond to what God has taught them in this session and throughout the whole series. Begin to pray together for your Nineveh – start to share God's love for his people. As the end of the study, each person will be given a gift – a plant to take home and look after. Remember, just as you join God in his work of nurturing the plant, he wants you to join him in his much greater work of sharing his amazing grace and love with all people.

FURTHER STUDY

If you want to be more involved in sharing God's concern for the nations, then start praying! An excellent information and prayer resource is *Operation World* by Patrick Johnstone. There is also a children's version of this book.

FOR FUTURE WEEKS

Review the life-lessons God taught Jonah and ask yourself:

▶ Am I developing as a world Christian?
▶ Am I telling people about the good news?
▶ Am I growing in my knowledge of God?
▶ Am I making prayer and repentance a priority?
▶ Am I growing in my sensitivity to God and his will?
▶ Am I being obedient to what God is calling me to do?
▶ Does what I say match up with what I do?

ACTIVITY PAGE

In the book of Jonah we are introduced to a God who is intimately concerned with the world, he knows what's going on, and he takes the initiative to intervene. This is not the picture many non-Christians or even Christians have of God. Imagine the following scenarios. Brainstorm as a group some possible responses.

▶ You are watching the news with a non-Christian friend. The newsreaders speaks about the events of September 11, 2001; the instability in the Middle East; further terrorist attacks etc. Your friend turns to you and says 'You can't possibly believe there's a God when you see the mess the world's in!'

▶ A child in your son's class at school was seriously injured in a freak car accident. The child's mother says to you, 'If God loved my son he would have protected him.'

▶ A new Christian is going through a difficult time at work. At housegroup you ask them whether they have prayed about the situation. They reply 'Yes, but nothing has changed yet. Anyway, God probably has bigger, more important issues to deal with right now.'

LEADERS' GUIDE

TO HELP YOU LEAD

You may have led a housegroup many times before or this may be your first time. Here is some advice on how to lead these studies:

▶ As a group leader, you don't have to be an expert or a lecturer. You are there to facilitate the learning of the group members – helping them to discover for themselves the wisdom in God's word. You should not be doing most of the talking or dishing out the answers, whatever the group expects from you!

▶ You do need to be aware of the group's dynamics, however. People can be quite quick to label themselves and each other in a group situation. One person might be seen as the expert, another the moaner who always has something to complain about. One person may be labelled as quiet and not be expected to contribute; another person may always jump in with something to say. Be aware of the different type of individuals in the group, but don't allow the labels to stick. You may need to encourage those who find it hard to get a word in, and quieten down those who always have something to say. Talk to members between sessions to find out how they feel about the group.

▶ The sessions are planned to try and engage every member in active learning. Of course you cannot force anyone to take part if they don't want to, but it won't be too easy to be a spectator. Activities that ask everyone to write down a word, or talk in twos, and then report back to the group are there for a reason. They give everyone space to think and form their opinion, even if not everyone voices it out loud.

▶ Do adapt the sessions for your group as you feel is appropriate. Some groups may know each other very well and will be prepared to talk at a deep level. New groups may take a bit of time to get to know each other before making themselves vulnerable, but encourage members to share their lives with each other.

▶ You probably won't be able to tackle all the questions in each session so decide in advance which ones are most appropriate to your group and situation.

▶ Encourage a number of replies to each question. The study is not about finding a single right answer, but about sharing experiences and thoughts in order to find out how to apply the Bible to people's lives. When brainstorming, don't be too quick to evaluate the contributions. Write everything down and then have a look to see which suggestions are worth keeping.

▶ Similarly encourage everyone to ask questions, to voice doubts and to discuss difficulties. Some parts of the Bible are difficult to understand. Sometimes the Christian faith throws up paradoxes. Painful things happen to us that make it difficult to see what God is doing. A housegroup should be a safe place to express all of this. If discussion doesn't resolve the issue, send everyone away to pray about it between sessions, and ask your minister for advice.

▶ Give yourself time in the week to read through the Bible passage and the questions. Read the Leaders' notes for the session, as different ways of presenting the questions are sometimes suggested. However, during the session don't be too quick to come in with the answer – sometimes people need space to think.

▶ Delegate as much as you like! The easiest activities to delegate are reading the text, and the worship sessions, but there are other ways to involve the group members. Giving people responsibility can help them own the session much more.

▶ Pray for group members by name, that God would meet with them during the week. Pray for the group session, for a constructive and helpful time. Ask the Lord to equip you as you lead the group.

THE STRUCTURE OF EACH SESSION
Feedback: find out what people remember from the previous session, or if they have been able to act during the week on what was discussed last time.

To set the scene: an activity or a question to get everyone thinking about the subject to be studied.

Bible reading: it's important to actually read the passage you are studying during the session. Ask someone to prepare this in advance or go around the group reading a verse or two each. Don't assume everyone will be happy to read out loud.

Questions and activities: adapt these as appropriate to your group. Some groups may enjoy a more activity-based approach; some may prefer just to discuss the questions. Try out some new things!

Worship: suggestions for creative worship and prayer are included, which give everyone an opportunity to respond to God, largely individually. Use these alongside singing or other group expressions of worship. Add a prayer time with opportunities to pray for group members and their families and friends.

For next week: this gives a specific task to do during the week, helping people to continue to think about or apply what they have learned.

For further study: suggestions are given for those people who want to study the themes further. These could be included in the housegroup if you feel it's appropriate and if there is time.

WHAT YOU NEED

A list of materials that are needed is printed at the start of each session in the Leaders' Guide. In addition you will probably need:

Bibles: the main Bible passage is printed in the book so that all the members can work from the same version. It will be useful to have other Bibles available, or to ask everyone to bring their own, so that other passages can be referred to.

Paper and Pens: for people who need more space than is in the book!

Flip chart: it is helpful to write down people's comments during a brainstorming session, so that none of the suggestions is lost. They may not be space for a proper flip chart in the average lounge, and having one may make it feel too much like a business meeting or lecture. Try getting someone to write on a big sheet of paper on the floor or coffee table, and then stick this up on the wall with blu-tack.

GROUND RULES

How do people know what is expected of them in a housegroup situation? Is it ever discussed, or do we just pick up cues from each other? You may find it helpful to discuss some ground rules for the housegroup at the start of this course, even if your group has been going a long time. This also gives you an opportunity to talk about how you, as the leader, see the group. Ask everyone to think about what they want to get out of the course. How do they want the group to work? What values do they want to be part of the group's experience; honesty, respect, confidentiality? How do they want their contributions to be treated? You could ask everyone to write down three ground rules on slips of paper and put them in a bowl. Pass the bowl around the group. Each person takes out a rule and reads it, and someone collates the list. Discuss the ground rules that have been suggested and come up with a top five. This method enables everyone to contribute fairly anonymously. Alternatively, if your group are all quite vocal, have a straight discussion about it!

NB – Not all questions in each session are covered, some are self-explanatory.

ICONS

 The aim of the session

 Engaging with the world

 Investigate what else the Bible says

 How does this apply to me?

 What about my church?

SESSION 1

MATERIALS

- Bible atlas, flip chart

TO SET THE SCENE

This is meant to be a light-hearted look at our childhood days. As this is the first session for your group, don't let the sharing time become too deep or cause any embarrassment for people. The point is that we all have a rebellious streak when the rules don't suit us. Unfortunately, this applies even when we're Christians and when the consequences of disobedience to God are much more serious.

1   Nineveh was an evil, violent city; it had a large population; an impressive army; was riddled with prostitution and witchcraft; had a huge trading capacity; and plenty of enemies.

2   God told Jonah to go five hundred miles east to Nineveh but he headed two thousand miles due west; virtually the length of the Mediterranean Sea, the span of the known world.

3   Amos said that because God had spoken he didn't have any option but to prophesy, Isaiah was obedient; even the pagan prophet Balaam recognised it was foolish to reject God's commission. Jonah is the only prophet recorded in Scripture who disobeyed God's call.

4   God's word comes to us primarily through the Bible. God may speak to us when we pray, in worship services, and through conversations with other people – but this will never contradict what he had already said in the Bible.

5   Jonah disobeyed because he knew that if the people repented, God would relent from sending punishment. He didn't want God's grace extending to Israel's enemies.

6   God spoke to Jonah throughout the book, he sent the storm, provided the fish, commanded it to spit Jonah out, relented from destroying the Ninevites, grew the vine, sent the worm and then the scorching wind.

7 a) We disobey for many reasons. For example, we think God isn't working on our behalf; we say we don't have the time or the gifts to get involved; we're frightened of the difficulties we may face if we obey and obedience often means stepping into the unknown.

b) Disobedience often affects our families as they live with the consequences of our decisions. At times, we see our mistakes being repeated by our children.

8 Essentially, Noah and Abraham obeyed not because what God asked them to do made sense, but because they trusted his character. They were in tune with God, they heard his voice, and they believed that, in contrast to them, God knew the big picture and had a plan.

9 a) Encourage people to be as honest as possible.

b) Discuss practical options. For example recognise what type of person you – are you a friendship-evangelism type of person, a confronter, can you strike up conversations with strangers? Recognise the opportunities you do have to share the gospel. Would it help to think through your testimony or how to explain the gospel?

10 Churches are often so busy with their congregations that there is little time or inclination for evangelism into difficult communities. Pray through whether your church needs to expand its vision for the Ninevehs on a local or worldwide perspective. If the answer is 'yes' how can you do this, given your existing commitments?

SESSION 2

TO SET THE SCENE

You can think of additional questions to test the sensitivity of your group members. The aim of this icebreaker is to start people thinking about how we measure our spiritual sensitivity to God. Even the most sensitive people can be insensitive to God. So how do we know whether we are listening, available and growing more like Christ?

1 Jonah slept, apparently oblivious to the fatal danger the passengers were in, whilst the pagan captain was the one interested in saving human life. Jonah continued to ignore God but the captain, for all his sailing expertise, knew that this was a time to cry out for divine help.

2 The sailors were reluctant to throw Jonah overboard, they wanted to preserve his life. In contrast, Jonah was prepared for Nineveh to face God's judgement. The sailors are eager to pray and offer sacrifices for their actions; they show awareness of divine power and intervention. They did not want to offend God whilst his own prophet clearly ignored him. The sailors didn't necessary abandon their beliefs in other gods but recognised that Jonah's God was in charge of this particular event.

3 Jonah states his impressive credentials. He claimed to worship the God of the sea and land and yet at the same time thought he could run away from him. His speech and actions don't measure up at this point.

4 These passages challenge us that our beliefs should make a difference to our behaviour: if they don't they're worthless (Jas. 2:14–26). As believers, God will judge us for what we have done (1 Cor 3:10–15). God can see the difference between empty ritual, which may fool others, and real dedication of the heart.

5 There are various issues to look at. Could we be more disciplined in our commitment to live out our spiritual lives? Could we ask a prayer partner to hold us accountable in the area of integrity? Perhaps in the area of giving or evangelism, we need to ask for God's strength to be obedient and live out our beliefs, even if we don't feel like it.

6 God provided the fish to rescue Jonah. This reminds us that even our most spectacular failures don't necessarily disqualify us from God's service. God longs for our obedience and intimate fellowship with him.

7 Encourage people to reflect on God's kindness to them in their lives. This often helps us see God and our own situation from a true perspective.

8 Our hearts easily get spiritually calloused and hardened towards God. It helps to keep short accounts with him, to confess our sins daily, attempting to see our sin as he does. As we do so, we see our need of him and his grace in our lives. Also we should spend time in prayer and reading the Bible, listening for God's voice and learning what concerns him so that we start to share his vision.

SESSION 3

MATERIALS NEEDED
▶ Flip chart or large sheets of paper for brainstorming session, pens

TO SET THE SCENE
We easily become discouraged about praying and forget what God has done on our behalf. Sharing these memories with each other could help inspire the group to keep on persevering in prayer.

1 Get the group to look closely at the text. Jonah was drowning (v2); he was hopelessly overwhelmed by the tidal waves (v3, 5); seaweed surrounded him (v5); he was on the bottom of the ocean bed (v6); he was clinging to life when God rescued him (v7).

2 Evidence for true repentance: he seems to have changed his attitude (v9) and obeys when he hears God's word a second time (3:3); he realises that God had punished him (v3 'You hurled me') but also that it was God who saved him (v1, 6); the fact God sent the fish would seem to indicate he accepted his prayer. Evidence he didn't fully repent: he uses 'I' a lot – his prayer is self-centred; he doesn't remember the pagan sailors he'd left behind; his quotes from the psalms seem a little artificial given the situation; even if he thought he meant his prayer, his heart attitude towards the Ninevites hadn't changed (chapter 4).

3 Whatever your views on the reality of Jonah's repentance, we are reminded of the need to be sincere in our prayers. God hears every one; our prayers should be God-centred; any promises of commitment need to be backed up with action.

4 Jonah refers to prayers going to the temple – directly to God's presence. In 2:4 perhaps the 'temple' is the one in Jerusalem, in 2:7 perhaps he's referring to the heavenly temple.

5 Our prayers go into the very presence of a holy God. Jesus intercedes before God on our behalf and presents our prayers to him. Every prayer is heard and remembered. The fact that God treasures our prayers so much should encourage us to keep on praying and if there is no 'positive' answer, to reflect whether God is saying 'no' or 'wait'. Perhaps we should also think about the seriousness of prayer, and avoid approaching God carelessly.

6 For Jonah it meant acknowledging that God was free to save the Ninevites; it was God's decision, not his. All that was required was his obedience. God did not have any favourites; he loved the entire world. For the Ninevites, it meant calling out for God to be merciful; they had no claims or right to be forgiven. We should appreciate God's intervention to save us as we couldn't save ourselves; it was entirely due to his grace. Also, we should remember that whilst we do our best to present the gospel fully in contemporary ways, ultimately it is God's Spirit moving in people's hearts alone that brings people to salvation.

7 Try and be creative here. We've all only got twenty-four hours in the day but it is how we utilise them that counts. Think about praying whilst you're in the car on the way to and from work, whilst you're doing the ironing, at the gym etc. But make sure you set aside regular focused times for prayer and Bible reading.

8 Don't groan about the status of prayer in the church: do something constructive. Become part of a prayer triplet, ask your minister if you could have days of prayer or encourage groups to pray for particular interests, such as the local school, government officials, the persecuted church and so on.

SESSION 4

MATERIALS NEEDED
▶ Tapes or CDs, music system and candles for worship

TO SET THE SCENE
Having to say 'sorry' can be a very difficult and many of us carry baggage from when we should have said 'sorry' and didn't; or when others should have apologised to us and didn't. This exercise is to help people focus on the topic without them feeling too exposed. If people have deeper issues with this topic, perhaps spend time dealing with them further into the study, or on an individual basis afterwards.

LEADERS' GUIDE

1 Repentance is more than a feeling. It is a change of mind, heart, will and direction. It means your life takes a U-turn: instead of going your own way, you go God's way and are marked by his values.

2 Jonah obeyed and went to Nineveh as God had commanded. The Ninevites didn't just believe God and pray (v5, 8); they demonstrated their repentance practically. They fasted, put on sackcloth, and changed their behaviour. Their earnestness is seen in that even the animals fasted!

3 God is patient because he speaks to Jonah again; he is loving, wanting even the Ninevites to be saved; he listens, responding to people's cry for mercy; he clearly delights in showing his grace because he relents in sending his wrath on this evil nation; he is compassionate; his anger isn't purposeless: it is against sin.

4 Our faith is strengthened as we see God at work, we know we're being obedient to God, we know we were in the right place at the right time, and we share God's joy.

5 Knowing the thrill of leading someone to Christ and what it does for our own spiritual life is a valid motivation. But there are others: sheer obedience, wholehearted service, and the fact that we don't know how much time we – or anyone else – has left.

6 The Lord's Prayer would indicate that confession should be a daily part of a believer's life (Lk 11:1–4). Regular repentance reminds us of God's grace towards us, our sinfulness, and our need of him. It keeps us focused on God and maintains a healthy relationship with him.

7 Your group may come up with many ideas here. For example, letting materialism invade the church, not looking after the poor, not pioneering social action, not opposing the decline of morality, not being a greater influence in society. Perhaps there is a particular action your church could take – doing a soup run for the homeless, asking social services if there are any individuals you could help. Perhaps it will be up to individuals in your group to change their own priorities. Discuss this together.

8 Think of practical ways you could demonstrate to your local community the grace of God. In what ways is your church salty – in what ways is it making people thirsty to know more about Jesus? What activities does your church do that compels people's interest in Christ? Are theses activities effective?

SESSION 5

MATERIALS NEEDED

▶ Paper and pens, flipchart or large sheets of paper

▶ CD or tapes and music system for worship time

TO SET THE SCENE

Be kind as you're describing each other! This exercise should help people start thinking along the theme of character traits. Perhaps you may also find that your perception of people is different to how they perceive themselves. This is a reminder to appreciate God for who he really is, not how we imagine him to be.

1 Jonah knew but did not appreciate God's compassion and his desire to save people. He hadn't grasped how sinful he'd been or God's grace towards him and so couldn't understand the universality of God's grace.

2 Often we emphasis one aspect of God's character to the exclusion of others: God's approachability rather than his holiness; his love rather than his hatred of sin; that he's our friend rather than our judge.

3 (a) Knowing God gives a greater richness to our understanding of Scripture and how the two Testaments interlink. Then we don't force what we read to fit our situation but we see it in the context of the bigger picture of salvation-history.

(b) When we sing 'I love you' we know who we're singing about and also why we love him.

4 As we sing songs/hymns or hear Scripture being read and expounded, we learn about God. This highlights the need to have a rich content to our material. We also learn about him from what we see in others.

5 Christians: we have higher expectations of them because we believe the Holy Spirit should make a difference to their behaviour and attitudes. Because expectations are so high, the hurt is greater when we're disappointed and consequently, it's hard to give them a second chance. Non-Christians: we're often judgemental about their lifestyles, we perceive them as 'other' to us, and any offer of grace or mercy means cultivating a friendship which demands time.

6 It is difficult to follow a sovereign God because it means he will often not do exactly as we would wish; our personal good is only part of the whole cosmic plan; it means that though we're special, we're not favoured by God more than others; it means his ways are unfathomable. It requires more faith to trust in a God who is free to act rather than predictable but, on the other hand, it means he is worth trusting because he is so much greater and in control than we are.

7 Review your church practice: is there anything that you could change; is there anything you should speak to your church leaders about?

SESSION 6

MATERIALS NEEDED
▶ Pen and paper, flip chart

▶ Plants

TO SET THE SCENE
This is just a fun exercise to discover how well you know each other's interests and ambitions. You might know each other well or there may be a few surprises! Just as we want to learn about our partner and friends and share their interests, the same should be true of our relationship with God. We can't claim to love God if we're not interested in sharing his passions and concerns.

1 Jonah was concerned about a plant which he didn't do anything to nurture, so surely he should appreciate that God would care even more passionately about saving the souls which he'd created.

2 Jonah was self-absorbed and selfish. He'd rather die than see God's love be shared with these pagans. He did not want to share God's heart for mission to those outside Israel.

3 Perhaps include words and phrases like: saving sinners; creating a people who would be devoted to him; proclaiming the gospel to the unlovable; calling the nations to himself; seeking the lost; to the ends of the earth. A relevant verse could be John 3:16.

4 We often lose sight of why we do certain activities and it is worth analysing how we can maximise their kingdom impact.

5 Perhaps answer this question in twos so that people spend longer reflecting together.

6 We each have a part to play in God's mission. Your mission-field could be your family, home, street, workplace or school. We need to start seeing our circumstances as opportunities to serve God, introduce gospel values and live as Christ would if he were in our shoes.

7 God's grace and mercy; God's love for the nations; God taking the initiative; God giving second chances; obedience to God's will; repentance.

8 Encourage people to be specific about what they have learnt and the areas in which they need to grow. Discuss together practical measures which individuals can out in place to develop spiritually.

WORSHIP

As this is the last session, allow a longer time for worship so that individuals can make their commitments to God.

FOR FURTHER READING

R T Kendall, *Jonah*, Hodder & Stoughton

Rosemary Nixon, *Jonah*, (IVP: The Bible speaks today series, 2003)

If you would like further information and resources, the following organisations may be of help. They will be able to tell you what is going on in your locality and how you can get involved: